SOLVE THIS!

W9-ART-065

St. Procopius School Library
005015

CONTENTS

A PUZZLE FOR MR. BROWN

Mr. Brown had a big dog. The dog
went everywhere with Mr. Brown.
On their way to the market,
they rowed across the river
in Mr. Brown's little dinghy.
There was just enough room
for Mr. Brown and the dog.

One day at the market,
Mr. Brown bought a lamb
and a big cabbage.

The dog felt hungry. It looked
at the lamb and licked its lips.

The lamb felt hungry. It looked
at the cabbage and thought how
tasty it would be.

The lamb looked at the cabbage.
The dog looked at the lamb.
Then they both looked at Mr. Brown.

When they came to the river,
Mr. Brown said, "I can take only
one of you across at a time.
What shall I do?"

"If I take the cabbage,
the dog might eat the lamb
while I am away. If I take the dog,
the lamb might eat the cabbage."

What should Mr. Brown do?
(Think about it, then turn the page.)

"First, I will take the lamb
across the river and leave
the cabbage with the dog,"
said Mr. Brown.

He rowed the lamb across
the river and left it on the
other side. Then he rowed back.

"What shall I take next?" he asked.

"Oh dear. If I take the dog, it might eat the lamb when I come back for the cabbage. If I take the cabbage, the lamb might eat it when I come back for the dog."

What should Mr. Brown do?
(Think about it, then turn the page.)

"I know," said Mr. Brown. "I will take the dog over to the other side and bring the lamb back."

He rowed the dog across and took the lamb back, leaving the dog on its own.

"Now I will take the cabbage to the other side of the river and leave the lamb behind."

He rowed the cabbage across and left it with the dog. Then he went back for the lamb.

So Mr. Brown managed
to get his dog, his lamb,
and his cabbage safely home.

CHINESE CHARACTERS

Long ago in China, there was
a four-eyed god named Cangjie.
He was in charge of keeping
all the records.

   At first, he kept track
of everything by tying knots
in ropes. It was tiring work.

One day, Cangjie saw an animal's footprints in the dirt. He thought that if people could recognize an animal from its footprints, they could look at picture-signs and learn what they stood for.

He began to draw everything
he saw. He made many simple
drawings. This was the beginning
of the Chinese written language.

Here are some Chinese
characters that are used today:

狗 dog　　　龜 turtle

早晨 morning　　河 river

太陽 sun　　　鳥 bird

爪 claws　　拖車 wagon

Now read this story:

THE DOG AND THE TURTLE

There was once a 狗
that was friends with a 龜.
Even though the 龜 was slow,
the 狗 would walk along
with it patiently.

The 龜 liked to spend the 早晨 swimming in the 河. The 狗 would lie down beside its friend and warm itself in the bright morning 太陽.

狗
dog

龜
turtle

早晨
morning

河
river

太陽
sun

鳥
bird

爪
claws

拖車
wagon

15

One day, a huge 鳥
saw the shiny shell of the 龜.
It flew down. The 鳥 stuck out
its 爪 and snatched up the 龜.

The 狗 barked and barked.
It growled and showed its teeth.
The 狗 chased the 鳥
across the field.

狗
dog

龜
turtle

早晨
morning

河
river

太陽
sun

鳥
bird

爪
claws

拖車
wagon

Finally, the 鳥 dropped the 龜,
and the 龜 fell to the ground.

The shell of the 龜 was cracked, and the 龜 hurt all over. The 狗 was mad at the 鳥.

狗
dog

龜
turtle

早晨
morning

河
river

太陽
sun

鳥
bird

爪
claws

拖車
wagon

The 狗 found a little 拖車
and helped the 龜 into it.
The 狗 pulled the 拖車
until they came to the 河.

20

The 狗 took the 龜
out of the 拖車.
It put the 龜 in the 河.
Slowly, the 龜 started to move.
The 狗 watched the 龜 swim
up and down in the 河.

狗
dog

龜
turtle

早晨
morning

河
river

太陽
sun

鳥
bird

爪
claws

拖車
wagon

21

In time, the 龜 healed.
From that day forward,
any time a 鳥 came near the 龜,
the 狗 would bark and bark.
   The 狗 was a true friend
to the 龜.

狗
dog

龜
turtle

早晨
morning

河
river

太陽
sun

鳥
bird

爪
claws

拖車
wagon

23

REBUS STORIES

Rebus stories are fun to make and read. Instead of writing the nouns, you can draw a picture.

 = cats

When you write a verb,
you can sometimes draw part
of it.

loo 👑 = looking

🗝 p = keep

You can also use numbers
or letters for a word.

R = are   4 = for

2 = to   ✖ = cross

U = you   y = why

Use this code to read the rebus story "The Old Man and the Bear":

 = man   r🥄ed = roared

= wolf   cl👁mb = climb

= reindeer   🐻's = bear's

= bear   = coat

loo👑 = looking   = would

= river   = not

= winter   = so

n👂 = near   = be

✖ = cross   2 = to

🆄 = you   4 = for

w💪 = warm   = food

👕s = coats   k👁nd = kind

= water   = sleep

= can   🔑p = keep

a✖ = across   = spring

👁 = I   y = why

't = can't   s = sleeps

THE OLD MAN AND THE BEAR

An old ___, a ___, a ___ ___,

and a ___ stood loo___

at the ___. ___ was n___.

"We must **X** the ___,"

said the old ___.

"**U** have w___ ___s,

but the cold ___ will kill me.

___, ___ **U** help me

a**X** the ___?"

27

"No," said the ,

"  't help U,"

and he swam a✖ the .

"  ," said the old ,

"  U help me?"

"No," said the  ,

"  't help U,"

and he swam a✖ the .

" help ," red the .

"Clmb on my back."

The old was carried

a the . He was dry,

and the 's thick

kept him w.

The and the

laughed at the .

" and ," said the old ,
who was really a god,

" help me, will

help . All , will

cold and will have 2 search

4 ."

"," he said, " were k nd

2 me, will k nd 2 .

All , will and your

will p w until

comes again."

And that is y the s

all .

SOLVE THIS WORD SEARCH

Hidden in this word search are fifteen words from the book.

C	A	B	B	A	G	E	M	C	Z
D	P	U	Z	Z	L	E	A	H	K
N	S	Y	N	T	S	R	R	A	E
E	L	U	R	U	U	E	K	R	I
I	S	U	F	Q	B	T	E	A	J
R	T	L	G	L	E	N	T	C	G
F	O	O	T	P	R	I	N	T	N
W	D	L	A	M	B	W	F	E	A
A	R	E	I	N	D	E	E	R	C

ANSWERS: cabbage, Cangjie, character, dog, footprint, friend, lamb, market, puzzle, rebus, reindeer, sun, turtle, winter, wolf

Puzzles, Riddles, AND Word Games

People have enjoyed solving puzzles and riddles since ancient times. In some folktales, winning a contest or saving a life may depend upon solving a riddle. Word games, such as word searches and crossword puzzles, are also enjoyed by many people.

You can make your own riddle, rebus story, or word search, and try it out on your friends.

ST. PROCOPIUS SCHOOL
1625 S. ALLPORT STREET
CHICAGO, IL 60608